KOROW

A Baby Chimpanzee's Story

Executive Producers, John Christianson and Ron Berry
Illustrator, Lara Gurin
Art Director and Book Designer, Eugene Epstein
Writer and Creative Director, Kathleen Duey
DVD Mastering and Editor, Stephanie Carlson
DVD Soundtrack and Song Composed and Produced by George Fogelman
DVD Audio Mixed and Mastered by Robert Cartwright and George Fogelman
DVD Video Narrator, Daniel Krasner
DVD Song, Sung by Ian Brininstool and George Fogelman
DVD Video Footage, the British Broadcasting Company
Production Manager, Doug Boggs

Distributed by Ideals Publications
A Guideposts Company
535 Metroplex Drive, Ste 250, Nashville, TN 37211

ISBN # 9780824918163
Printed and bound in China

KOROW

A Baby Chimpanzee's Story

It was raining hard. The forest smelled like wet earth and flowers. My mother and I sat close together, as always.

We were all hungry, waiting for the rain to stop.

I heard chimpanzees from another family calling.
One of my mother's sisters answered. Then it was quiet again.
When the rain slowed to a drizzle my mother helped me
onto her back. It was time to go look for breakfast.

The sun came out as we followed the river. I didn't know where we were going, but I was sure my mother did. I just hoped we would find food soon!

My mother and her sisters all crossed the river without getting wet, swinging above it on tree branches. I hung on tight, looking down at the water below us.

Once we were on the other side,
I heard screeching and looked up.
Two of my friends had followed their
mothers, swinging through the
branches on their own.

I slid off my mother's shoulders.
I wanted to go play with my friends,
but she wouldn't let me. Maybe she
didn't think I was big enough.
She settled me on her back again.
Then she hurried to catch up
with the family.

I smelled the ripe fruit before
I saw it. I waited while my mother
climbed up to pick enough for both
of us. It was sweet and wonderful.
Everyone in my family wanted more!

We all ate so much that the only fruit left was at the top of the tree. The highest branches were too small to hold my mother—or any of the other adults. So she climbed down. Everyone did.

My mother and her friends were full and a little sleepy. They sat close together and began to groom each other. They do it all the time—no one likes to have fleas and ticks in their fur. Usually, I play with my friends nearby when my mother is busy, but that day...

I had a better idea.

I started up the tree.
I could see the endless
blue sky through the leaves.

Halfway to the top, I stopped and looked back at my family. I had never been that high before without my mother. I was a little scared, but I knew I could get down.

I stared at the fruit. The branches were really thin and they were swaying in the breeze. I knew I would have to be very careful. I started climbing again.

As I reached out, I was a little scared. But I got the fruit! I was so happy. I had climbed higher than I ever had before, higher than any of my friends. It was the sweetest fruit I had ever tasted.

After I finished, I looked out over the forest.

I could hear birds calling from the treetops

around me and the sound of the distant river.

I could hear my friends playing, too, far below.

I climbed down,
hooting and calling to my friends.
By the time I got there, they were
chasing each other around the tree.

We had so much fun!

*T*hen it was time to leave. My mother started to lift

me up onto her back, but I wouldn't let her.

I had climbed the tree by myself. I had gone higher

than anyone else. There was no reason for her to carry me.

When she started walking, I followed her.

We walked a long way and I got tired! When my family stopped to rest, I napped with my mother.

When we went on, she
walked with her sister.
I ran to play with my friends.
She kept glancing at me
to make sure I was all right, but
she let me play until the sun
was almost down!

That night, I helped my mother make a leafy nest.
There were stars glittering through the treetops. I knew
the whole sky was full of stars and that it was really big.
I had seen it! A breeze made the leaves whisper and sigh,
and my mother held me close as I went to sleep.

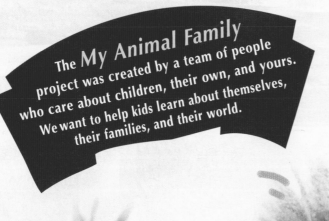

The **My Animal Family** project was created by a team of people who care about children, their own, and yours. We want to help kids learn about themselves, their families, and their world.

The Illustrated Book

Our beautifully illustrated books are written with care.
Each story is about the realistic adventures of a wild baby animal
and is an accurate portrait based upon current behavioral research.
Every story gives parents and grandparents opportunities to talk to
their children about home, life and family.

The Activity Website

The **My Animal Family** creative team includes game and website designers, too. We have built a **safe**, fun place for kids to play "animal" activities online. At **MAFKidsClub.com**, children will find their favorite animal friends in their native habitats. Set in arctic snow, tropical forests, oceans and deserts, the games help pre-readers get ready for school and keep beginning readers happy and busy. Games are leveled so that each visitor can build confidence and master basic skills. The creative team has worked hard to make the website friendly, fun, interesting, and safe for your kids.

The Live-Action Animal DVD

Every book includes a live-action DVD that features **award-winning BBC** wildlife video footage. Carefully edited for young children, the footage gives them a glimpse into the reality of each baby animal s life. Kids learn about the cooperation that helps animal families survive and thrive, and about the habitats where they live.

MY ANIMAL FAMILY®

Welcome to the Club!

Leo goes exploring, then has to find his way back to his family.

LEO — A Baby Lion's Story

Korow learns to climb high enough to pick her own fruit.

KOROW — A Baby Chimpanzee's Story

Ella helps protect a newborn baby elephant in danger.

ELLA — A Baby Elephant's Story

Nanuq saves his bossy brother from a foolish mistake.

NANUQ — A Baby Polar Bear's Story

My Animal Family is a new kind of children's club. With books to read, DVDs to enjoy, games to play, puzzles to solve and adventures to share, it's the kind of club every child dreams of... *"where the fun and good times never stop."*

Membership begins with the purchase of a beautifully illustrated storybook. Every story in the series is captivating and stars a baby animal in a realistic, family adventure... animal families that include elephants, lions, chimpanzees, polar bears, and many more...

Use the secret passcode on your membership card to explore *www.MAFKidsClub.com*. There are no advertisements or fees.